A Study Of The Propagation And Interception Of Energy In Wireless Telegraphy, Part 1

Charles Aaron Culver

In the interest of creating a more extensive selection of rare historical book reprints, we have chosen to reproduce this title even though it may possibly have occasional imperfections such as missing and blurred pages, missing text, poor pictures, markings, dark backgrounds and other reproduction issues beyond our control. Because this work is culturally important, we have made it available as a part of our commitment to protecting, preserving and promoting the world's literature. Thank you for your understanding.

# A STUDY OF THE PROPAGATION AND INTER-CEPTION OF ENERGY IN WIRELESS TELEGRAPHY. PART I

By CHARLES A. CULVER

[Reprinted from the PHYSICAL REVIEW, Vol. XXV, No 3, September, 1907]

THESIS

PRESENTED TO THE FACULTY OF PHILOSOPHY OF THE UNIVERSITY OF PENN-
SYLVANIA IN PARTIAL FULFILMENT OF THE REQUIREMENTS
FOR THE DEGREE OF PH. D.

1907

[Reprinted from the PHYSICAL REVIEW, Vol. XXV., No. 3, September, 1907.]

# A STUDY OF THE PROPAGATION AND INTERCEPTION OF ENERGY IN WIRELESS TELEGRAPHY. PART I.

BY CHARLES A. CULVER.

## PURPOSE.

FROM time to time our own and various foreign governments have issued numerous patents covering various types of antennæ or aërial systems, which have been designed for the purpose of radiating or receiving electromagnetic waves. While there has been some quantitative work done on the efficiency of these various types, the investigations have been conducted largely along commercial lines. The writer is not aware that any extended quantitative research in this direction has been carried out under conditions permitting of delicate and highly accurate measurement. Aside from the practical bearing which the results of such a research might have, it was believed that a study of the action of these various types might possibly yield data which would throw some light upon one or more of the undetermined theoretical problems at present existing in this field. With this end in view it was *the purpose of this investigation to make a study of the relative efficiency of several different types of receiving systems when used under various conditions.* In so far as this paper treats of aërials or antennæ it has to do with conditions at the receiving station only. In a future paper we hope to investigate several radiating systems in a similar manner.

## APPARATUS EMPLOYED.

*Sending Station.* — The equipment at the power station consisted of a transformer, $T$, Fig. 1, $a$, two inductance coils, $L_1$ and $L_2$, a spark gap, $G_1$ and a battery of six Leyden jars, $C_1$. A single insulated wire[1] ten meters in length served as a radiating system.

[1] Whenever wire is referred to hereafter, unless otherwise specified, insulated copper wire No. 10 bearing the trade name "Fire and Water Proof" is meant.

Seven and eight tenths meters of this wire were supported in vertical position by means of a specially constructed high tension insulator. The transformer employed was rated to deliver 25,000 volts when operating on a 104 volt 60 cycle circuit. The voltage, however, was cut down to about 5,000 by means of an adjustable rheostat in

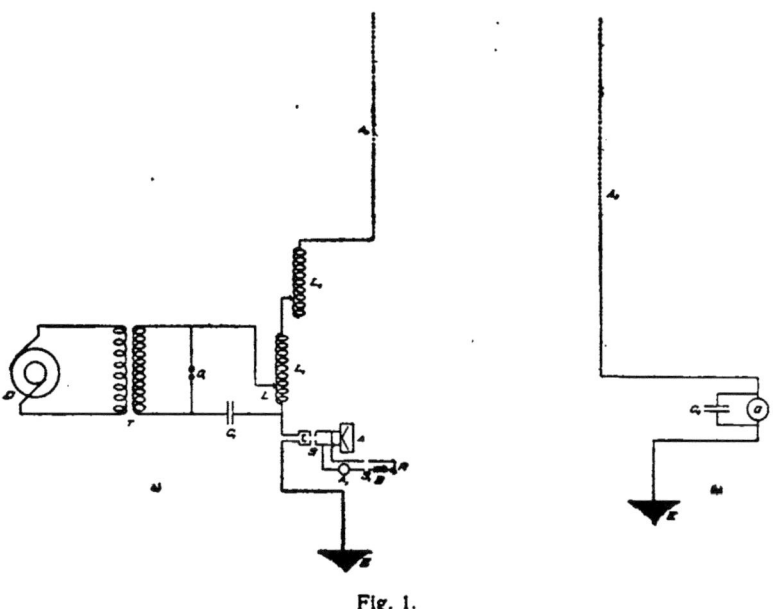

Fig. 1.

series with the primary. Power was secured from commercial mains. The Leyden jars composing the capacity, $C_1$, were specially constructed for high tension work and were worked in parallel, their combined capacity being 0.00837 M-F. The two inductance coils, $L_1$ and $L_2$, consisted of 23 turns of No. 9 bare copper wire (B.S.G.) wound on rectangular wooden frames 30.5 cm. square, the pitch of the winding, being 1.3 cm. One of these coils, $L_1$, served as on auto-transformer and the other, $L_2$, as an auxiliary tuning coil. The spark gap, $G_1$, was located on the top of the coil, $L_1$, and consisted of two extremely hard and highly polished steel balls 2.54 cm. in diameter, resting on the top of two short upright pieces of brass tubing 1.3 cm. internal diameter. One of these brass supports was adjustable, thus permitting the length of the spark gap to be varied. A spark length of 1 or 2 mm. was employed. Such an arrangement is probably as satisfactory as any form of gap for the reason that such steel balls are very refractory and may be readily changed or polished. Signals were made by opening and closing a switch in the primary circuit of the transformer, $T$. The power in the commercial mains from which our energy supply was taken varied between 3 and 4 per cent. in voltage. Various forms of earth connections were tried and the one ultimately employed was not used because it permitted the greatest amount of energy to be radiated from the sending station, for it did not, but for other reasons which will become obvious as we proceed. A hole $2 \times 4 \times 6$ feet was excavated in the earth. In the bottom of this hole a piece of gas pipe, 6 feet long, was driven until but 2 or 3 inches remained above the bottom of the hole. A sheet of galvanized iron $2 \times 8$ feet, having a hole in the middle large enough to admit the gas pipe, was placed in the excavation. This covered the bottom of the hole and extended upward on either of two sides for some 2 or 3 feet. The gas pipe passed through the hole in the middle of the metal sheet, extending above the same for 2 or 3 inches. Bare copper wire No. 9 (B.S.G.) led from the auto-transformer to earth, being soldered to the plate and also to the pipe. Such an arrangement was found to work reasonably well, though not so satisfactorily as a "ground" made by soldering the earth wire to gas or water pipes in the building. Both the ground and antenna wires were led out of the building through heavy porcelain insulators.

In order to determine when the two oscillating systems at the sending station were in resonance with each other, a specially constructed hot-wire ammeter was inserted between the inductance, $L_1$, and the earth. Fleming and others have pointed out that the ordinary commercial hot-wire ammeter will not give correct readings when operating on a high frequency circuit. This is due of course to the fact that with any instrument operating upon the shunt principle, the amount of current which will pass through the instrument proper is a function of the frequency. Since in the process of bringing two parts of any high frequency alternating circuit into resonance the frequency of one or both of the related circuits changes, therefore an instrument to give correct readings, even though only maximum current is desired, must be independent of the frequency and wave form. In this investigation an instrument was constructed along the lines suggested by Professor Fleming.[1]

Referring to Fig. 2, $WW_1$ is a No. 34 copper wire 32 cm. long, stretched between two binding posts, $BB_1$. This wire is drawn taut by a silk thread, $TT_1$, 16 cm. in length, fastened to its middle part

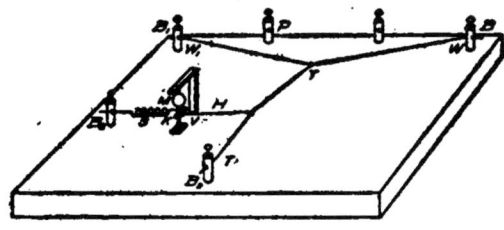

Fig. 2.

by means of a small double hook made of glass, the copper wire slipping freely through the glass hook. The end, $T_1$, of the above thread is fastened to a short piece of heavy brass wire which is held in place by a binding post, $B_2$. $V$ is a short steel shaft having conical points at either end and supported by suitable brass bearings fastened to the base of the instrument, which is of wood. This shaft carries a mirror, $M$, fastened to it by any convenient means. The shaft carries a short brass projection, $K$, having two small holes near its free extremity. A piece of fine piano wire, $H$, 3 cm. long having a loop at either end connects this brass lever to the middle of the thread, $TT_1$. The system thus formed is kept taut by means of spring, $S$, attached to the brass lever, $K$, and to a short piece of heavy brass wire which is held in place by means of a binding post, $B_3$. Any expansion of the wire, $WW_1$, due to current passing through the same will result in a movement of the mirror, $M$, which may be read by means of telescope and scale in the usual manner. The tension on the wire and the normal position of the mirror is modified by means of the adjustments possible at $B_2$ and $B_3$. A light wooden box enclosed the working parts of the instrument. By suitable choice of the wire, $WW$, various ranges and degrees of sensibility can be secured. Such an instrument gives the root-mean-square value of the current passing through it, and is independent

[1] The Principles of Electric Wave Telegraphy, p. 142.

of the frequency and wave form. Fig. 3 shows a typical calibration curve of the instrument, made by means of a standard Weston instrument and direct current. A series of tests extending over several days, under varying conditions of temperature and humidity, showed that the instrument held its calibration to a fair degree of accuracy. However, to avoid any possible changes due to external conditions we did not depend upon the calibration curve but used the instrument as a comparator. A reference to Fig. 2 will indicate how this was accomplished. The hot-wire ammeter was so arranged that it

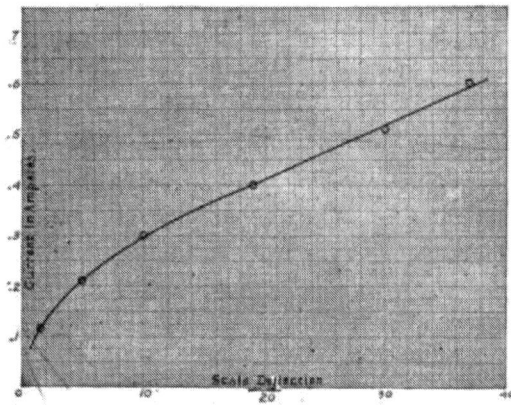

Fig. 3.

could be switched into the oscillating circuit at the same point at all times. After the mean-square value of the oscillating current had been read the ammeter was switched out of the oscillating circuit and into a direct current circuit in series with a finely adjustable rheostat and a standard Weston ammeter. The direct current was then adjusted until a deflection of the hot-wire instrument was secured equal to that caused by the oscillating current. The reading of the Weston instrument then gave the root-mean-square value of the high frequency current. The instrument was utilized not only to determine the conditions of maximum current in the inductance circuit but also to serve as a check on the constancy of the energy output at the sending station whenever it was impracticable to repeat any given set of measurements. After the two circuits at the sending station were brought into resonance the relation of the parts was not changed during the remainder of the experiments.

## Receiving Station.

The receiving station was equipped with various forms of antennæ; two adjustable oil condensers, $C_2$, arranged in parallel and shunted about the energy-measuring instrument; an oscillating current galvanometer, $G$, which served to measure the energy intercepted by the various receiving systems; an earth connection, $E$, similar to that described for the sending station. Fig. 1, $b$, illustrates the connections at the receiving station. The oil condensers consisted of two sets of sectorial-shaped brass plates, one set of which revolved about an axis set near one edge of the movable plates and close to the fixed sectors. A pointer attached to the axis moved over a scale graduated in circular degrees. Several such condensers were at our disposal, having been constructed from plans and specifications given by Clyde C. Swayne in an article which appeared in the American Electrician for September, 1905. Each condenser had a maximum capacity of .00211 M-F., and a minimum of .000771 M-F. Such condensers were found to serve admirably for delicate tuning in wireless circuits.

The energy-measuring instrument was an oscillating current galvanometer modelled along the lines suggested by Fleming and developed by Northrup[1] and Pierce.[2] In general the mechanical construction did not differ materially from the instrument now sold by the Leeds & Northrup Co., except that only one coil was used and the damping magnet was omitted. In detail the instrument as used in this investigation consisted of a small coil composed of 45 turns of No. 36 D.S.C. copper wire wound on a hollow hard rubber bobbin 7 mm. internal diameter. Directly in front of this coil was suspended by a very fine quartz fiber a small silver disc 6 mm. in diameter and .2 mm. thick. The suspension fiber was fastened to the metal disc by shellacing both to a delicate glass stem. The glass stem also carried a tiny mirror. The system thus composed was enclosed in a square hard rubber case having glass windows front and back. The suspension tube was of brass. Brass levelling screws completed the instrument. A non-inductive shunt might have been employed to vary the sensibility of the galvanometer;

---

[1] Electrical World, December 18, 1898.
[2] PHYSICAL REVIEW, Vol. 19, p. 202.

however, only one degree of sensibility was used throughout the experiments. Northrup and Pierce have shown that for small angles the deflection of such an instrument is proportional to the square of the current. The deflections were read by means of telescope and scale placed at a distance of 83 cm. from the galvanometer.

The two stations were 47 meters apart, the sending antenna being located on the north side of one building and the various receiving systems on the south side of an adjacent building, the two buildings constituting the Randall Morgan Laboratory thus being located between the two stations.

### WAVE-LENGTH MEASUREMENTS.

In order to measure the two wave-lengths emitted by the transmitting station, a wave-measuring apparatus was set up consisting of one of the adjustable oil condensers before referred to; a small inductance coil 21 cm. in diameter, carrying 9 turns of low resistance wire; a Duddell thermo-galvanometer in series with the condenser and inductance.[1] The inductance of the small helix and leads to the same measured by the Fleming-Anderson method was .0642 milli-henrys. This wave-measuring system was set up in the same room with the sending apparatus about 2 m. distant from the same. By means of such an arrangement the wave-length could be measured without the wave-meter circuit exerting any influence upon the system whose wave was being tested. The action of the thermo-galvanometer indicated that it would have been possible to perform the experiment with the wave-meter at even a much greater distance from the transmitting system. The wave-meter circuit was brought into resonance with the sending circuit by adjusting the oil condenser. It was found possible to secure very sharp resonance, a change of .5 of 1 per cent. in the capacity resulting in a falling off of at least 10 per cent. in the current as indicated by the galvanometer. This meant that a change in capacity of nine millionths of

[1] As this investigation is in progress we note the appearance of a paper by Professor Pierce (PHYSICAL REVIEW, Vol. 24, p. 152) in which the author describes the use of a similar device for measuring frequencies. Professor Pierce employs an oscillation galvanometer where we use the Duddell instrument. We believe the thermo-galvanometer to be somewhat superior for this purpose in that it is more dead beat and at the same time is amply sensitive for the purpose.

a microfarad was readily detectable. Advantage was taken of this fact later in measuring certain small values of capacity by means of an obvious substitution method. As was to be expected, the galvanometer indicated two current maxima, one with .001464 M-F., another with .001079 M-F.

Fleming has developed the working formula

$$n = \frac{5 \times 10^6}{\sqrt{LC}},$$

where $n$ represents the frequency, $L$ the inductance in centimeters and $C$ the capacity in microfarads. If we substitute in this equation the well-known relation

$$n = \frac{V}{\lambda},$$

where $V$ is the velocity of propagation and $\lambda$ the wave-length, we obtain the convenient expression

$$\lambda = 6 \times 10^3 \sqrt{LC}.$$

Substituting in this equation the values given above for $L$ and $C$ we get

$$\lambda_1 = 6 \times 10^3 \sqrt{64,200 \times .001464} = 581.7 \text{ meters},$$

$$\lambda_2 = 6 \times 10^3 \sqrt{64,200 \times .001079} = 499.2 \text{ meters}.$$

Thus it will be seen that the wave-lengths employed were comparable with those used for commercial purposes, the wave-length of the navy being 425 m.

### EFFECTS OF EARTH RESISTANCE.

*Preliminary Experiments.* — During the course of some preliminary experiments conducted at the beginning of this investigation, it was observed that with the receiving apparatus grounded by connecting to a piece of buried wire netting and the sending apparatus grounded to gas or steam pipes, the deflection of the galvanomete was four times what it was when the sending station was grounded to similar pieces of netting. When the receiving station was also grounded to pipes, the transmitting station being earthed through piping, the deflection at the receiving station was ten times what it was when both stations were earthed to buried netting. If the transmitting station were grounded to the plate and the receiving apparatus grounded first to the plate and then to the pipes in turn, little, if any, difference in the amount of energy received resulted. From these experiments it is apparant that the earth connections play a highly important part in the transmission of energy in wireless telegraph operations, particularly the "ground" at the transmitting station. While this fact is not new such marked differences as those observed when shown by careful measurements led the writer to try some experiments having to do with the effect earth resistance *between* stations might possibly have upon the quantity of energy transmitted. Accordingly the two stations were grounded to the two large galvanized iron earth plates and a wire run between the two stations, connecting to the earth leads where they enter the ground. Between the two stations this wire was insulated from the earth. In series with this wire was an adjustable non-inductive resistance. Thus there was arranged a variable resistance in parallel with the earth. With a constant supply of energy being radiated from the sending station, readings were made at the the receiving station with the parallel-earth-wire *disconnected* at both ends and then again with the variable resistance *connected* in parallel with the earth. While the energy received as shown by the relative deflections of the galvanometer was greater as the earth resistance was decreased, the results were not wholly concordant.

The experiment was next tried of placing several wires between the two stations so arranged that various combinations might be introduced in parallel with the earth. These wires were insulated from the earth except at the points where they connected to the earth leads where these leads entered the ground. To reduce the amount of energy received in order to bring the same within the range of the galvanometer without employing a shunt, a vertical receiving antenna 1.3 m. long was employed. The system thus constituted was brought into resonance with the sending station by adjusting the oil condensers shunted about the galvanometer. (This method of tuning was employed in all the experiments of this research.) By means of a Wheatstone bridge, a buzzer and a telephone the resistance of the earth between the two earth plates was measured. Similarly the resistance between these two points was measured when 1, 2, 3, . . . 6 wires were in parallel with the earth. Readings were also taken of the relative amounts of energy received under these various conditions. The amount of energy received increased materially as the earth resistance between the two stations was decreased. Table I. embodies the results of this experiment. In Fig. 4 the earth resistance between the two stations is plotted against galvanometer deflection (current square).

TABLE I.

| No. of Wires in Parallel with Earth. | Resistance Between Earth Plates, Ohms. | Gal. Deflection (Current Square). | No. of Wires in Parallel with Earth. | Resistance Between Earth Plates, Ohms. | Gal. Deflection (Current Square). |
|---|---|---|---|---|---|
| 0 | 90.0 | 4.0 | 4 | 17.0 | 117.0 |
| 1 | 74.7 | 38.5 | 5 | 14.0 | 128.0 |
| 2 | 34.7 | 78.0 | 6 | 11.7 | 140.0 |
| 3 | 22.9 | 102.0 | | | |

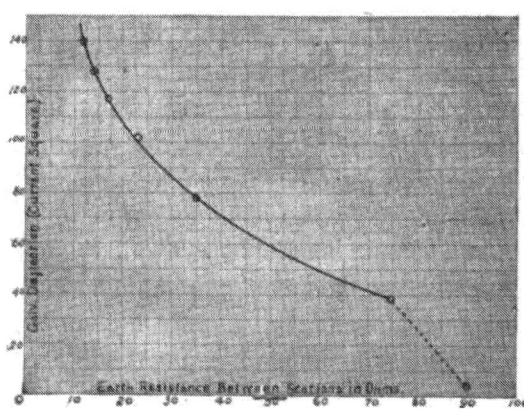

Fig. 4.

To further test the matter of earth resistance the wires above referred to were removed and a bare copper wire, No. 32, was strung out loosely on the damp ground and connected to the earth leads as in the above case. Immediately before this latter wire was put in place a mean reading was secured of the energy received, and as it was not practicable to repeat the test, a note was made of the reading of the antenna current at the sending station. When the wire was placed upon the ground as indicated above a mean reading of the received energy was made, and the galvanometer deflection proved to be 4.7 times the value when no wire connected the stations. The ratio between the current received in each case was nearly 2.2. The hot-wire ammeter at the sending station read slightly lower at the close of the experiment than at the beginning. Reference to the above facts will be made later in the paper.

HORIZONTAL ANTENNÆ.

An antenna was next constructed by supporting a wire 14.65 m. long in a horizontal position by means of porcelain insulators fastened to stakes driven in the ground. The mean height of this

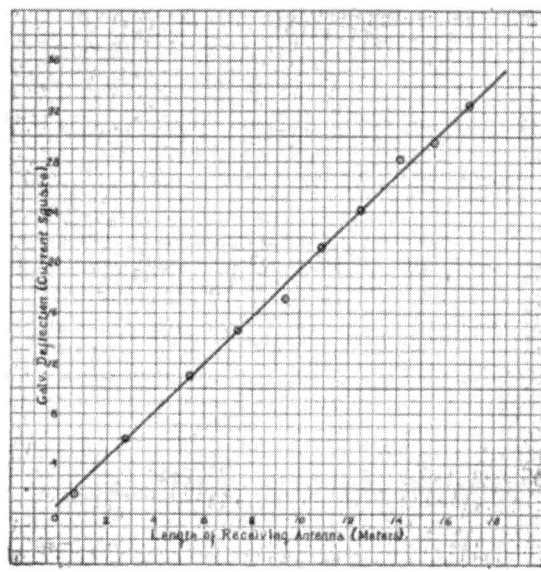

Fig. 5.

wire above the earth was .7 m. Since the receiving apparatus was located in a basement room, the permanent horizontal portion of antenna ($H$, Fig. 6) which led from the table containing the receiving apparatus to the exterior of the building was on a line with the horizontal antenna above referred to, thus making a total length of 16.8 m. Since it has been shown by Marconi, Fleming and others that such a horizontal antenna is most efficient when its free end is pointing directly away from the sending station, the above wire was placed in this position, the direction being determined first approximately by experiment and afterwards by means of a theodolite.

After the system thus established was brought into resonance with the sending station, which in this case was grounded to gas piping, the receiving station being connected to the earth plate, readings of the galvanometer deflections were taken as various portions of the horizontal receiving antenna were cut off. After any portion of the antenna was removed the system was again tuned to resonance. Table II. gives the result of this experiment. In Fig. 5 galvanometer deflections are plotted against length of receiving antenna. Though some of these points do not lie exactly on the curve, yet other data taken confirms the fact that *in the case of a horizontal antenna under the conditions with which we worked the square of the current received is proportional to the length of the antenna.*

TABLE II.

| Shunted Capacity Necessary to Effect Resonance. | Length of Horizontal Receiving Antenna. | Gal. Deflection. | Shunted Capacity Necessary to Effect Resonance. | Length of Horizontal Receiving Antenna. | Gal. Deflection. |
|---|---|---|---|---|---|
| 0.001559 m-f. | 16.80 meters. | 32.5 | 0.001600 m-f. | 9.40 meters. | 17.2 |
| 0.001571 " | 15.50 " | 29.5 | 0.001609 " | 7.40 " | 14.7 |
| 0.001581 " | 14.20 " | 28.2 | 0.001613 " | 5.40 " | 11.0 |
| 0.001591 " | 12.50 " | 24.2 | 0.001615 " | 2.75 " | 6.0 |
| 0.001593 " | 10.90 " | 21.2 | 0.001617 " | 0.65 " | 1.6 |

EFFECT OF ORIENTATION ON VARIOUS FORMS OF ANTENNÆ.

*Capacity-areas.*—To test the effects of orientation on different forms of antenna several types were constructed and tested. The first form experimented with consisted of a capacity-area 1 m. square made by tacking a piece of sheet tin to a wooden frame and supporting this by means of a metal rod passing through porcelain insulators attached to the supporting frame-work. The rod serving as an axis was supported by a wooden tripod. 1.05 m. of wire, nearly horizontal, connected this capacity-area to the permanent antenna lead ($H$, Fig. 6), the wire being soldered to the middle of the bottom edge of the tin. This capacity-area was supported at a height of 70 cm. above the ground at the point where the tripod stood and at a height of 16 cm. above the mean level of the ground between the two stations. By thus placing the area close to the ground it was possible to eliminate any effect due to any vertical wire leading to the same. Fig. 6 shows the general arrangement of parts in this and several succeeding experiments. The arrange-

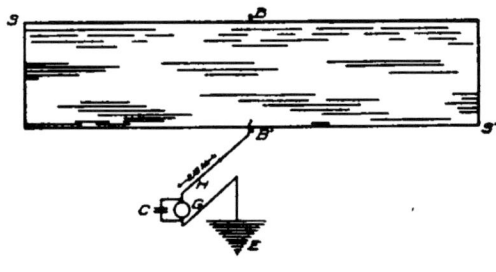

Fig. 6.

ment indicated permitted of rotating the capacity-area about a vertical axis. After bringing the system into resonance with the sending station, it was found that *the amount of energy received was the same for all planes of orientation about a vertical axis.*

The same area was next arranged in such a manner that orientation about a horizontal axis was possible. Other conditions were the same as in the previous case except that the area was supported 25 cm. above the mean level of the ground, and a vertical wire 75 cm. in length connected the middle of the tin sheet to the short horizontal lead $H$ before mentioned.

Readings of the energy received were made for various angles as the capacity-area was rotated about its horizontal axis. The mean of a number of readings showed that the area when in a vertical position produced a galvanometer deflection 5.6 per cent. (current 2.7 per cent.) greater than when horizontal. The difference between the maximum and minimum values is so small that it was not deemed of value to insert readings for intermediate angles.

Since the above results obtained on rotating the capacity-area about a vertical axis do not agree with the results obtained by Dr. De Forest,[1] it was decided to test the matter further. Accordingly

[1] "With a mechanism of this character having a collecting-screen 6 × 15 feet in size, I have been able to locate with certainty a transmitting-station seven miles distant within

a "collecting-screen" 4.17 × .71 m. was made of tin plates soldered together and fastened to suitable frame-work. The general arrangement of support was the same as for the smaller area (see Fig. 6), the center of the screen being 90 cm. above the earth at the point of support. A wire nearly horizontal, 2.67 m. in length, connected the middle of the lower edge of the metal surface to the lead, $H$. The screen was free to rotate about a vertical axis at its middle point.

After resonance was effected readings of energy received were made for various angles of rotation. *In this case a difference of 4.6 per cent. in the galvanometer deflection (current 2.4 per cent.) was found to exist, the greater amount of energy being received when the collecting-screen was broadside on to the waves.* Intermediate values are not recorded here. The above difference is by no means as great as that recorded by the investigator above referred to. It is to be remembered however that Dr. De Forest used the relative loudness of sounds in a telephone receiver as judged by the human ear as a means of determining the amount of energy received for various positions of his collecting-screens. It can scarcely be said that such equipment permitted of accurate quantitative measurements. Nevertheless it is possible that the same law does not obtain for both short and long distances.

## HELIX.

To test the effects of orientation upon an open circuited coil of large diameter when utilized as a receiving system a helix was constructed by winding two complete turns of wire about a wooden frame 1.5 m. square. This helix had an inductance of .040982 milli-henrys (Fleming-Anderson method). The helix thus made was supported and insulated as in the case of the small capacity-area, the free ends of the wire being at the middle of the lower edge of the coil. 1.7 m. of wire connected one end of the helix to the lead, $H$. The helix was so arranged as to permit of rotation about a central vertical axis. When resonance was secured in the usual manner energy readings were noted for various planes of orientation.

10 degrees, the transmitting-station being one designed for signal-transmitting purposes."
U. S. Patent No. 771,818, October 11, 1904, line 94.

*It was found that such an open circuited helix collected an equal amount of energy in all positions.*

The experiment was next tried of breaking the ground connection at the receiving station and in its place making a connection to the remaining free end of the helix above described, thus making a closed oscillating system without earth connections. In the case last outlined the galvanometer showed a deflection of 87.5 mm. With the closed helix just described placed tangential to the wave front the deflection was only 5 mm., and when the helix was turned through 90 degrees so as to have its plane normal to the wavefront the deflection was so small as to be scarcely readable. *The energy received by a closed helix apparently does not follow the same law as that of the open coil.* These results are somewhat surprising for if we assume the presence of a free Hertzian wave we would expect the open circuited helix to show a difference on orientation as well as the closed circuited coil.

### Screened Vertical Antenna.

The foregoing experiments gave rise in the mind of the writer to the thought that possibly the greater portion, if not all, of the energy transmitted in wireless telegraph operations is propagated by means of electric oscillations *through the surface of the earth and not by means of the free ether surrounding the same.*

With this thought in mind the following experiment was devised. Two vertical antennæ each consisting of a single wire 6.2 m. in length were erected 17 cm. apart, and were so arranged at the base that either could be quickly coupled to the lead, $H$. One of these vertical antennæ was then shielded from the free Hertzian waves by placing about it a metal cylinder made of tin, the cylinder being 10 cm. in diameter and 6.2 m. long. The enclosed wire hung freely within the metal tube which was insulated from the earth. Resonance was separately effected for both open and enclosed antennæ. On two different occasions several series of readings were taken in alternate groups, the results for the two tests agreeing within less than .1 of 1 per cent. The shielded antenna produced a mean galvanometer deflection 9.3 per cent. less than the unscreened system. This is equivalent to a difference of 4.9 per cent. in the value of the current in the two cases. The results of this experiment will be discussed elsewhere.

RELATIVE EFFICIENCY OF VARIOUS ENERGY-COLLECTING SYSTEMS.

We were now in a position to carry out a series of experiments designed to determine the relative efficiency as energy-gathering devices of the several types of antennæ now in commercial use. One or two original systems were also devised and tested. The two vertical single-wire antennæ described in the last experiment were so arranged as to permit of being connected at both the top and bottom, thus four different modifications of one system were possible. The metal cylinder used to enclose the vertical antenna of the last experiment was also suitably arranged to be used as a receiving system. The several cases are illustrated diagrammatically in Fig. 7 and will be referred to hereafter as systems $A$, $B$, $C$, $D$ and $E$, as indicated in the drawing.

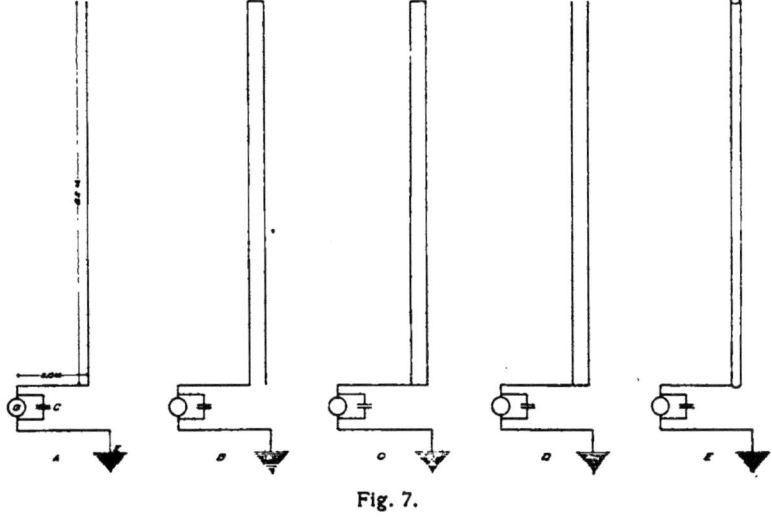

Fig. 7.

After the capacity[1] of the vertical portions of these systems was measured the systems were each in turn compared as energy-gathering devices with the simple vertical wire, $A$, taken as a standard. In these tests the readings for any given comparison were made by

[1] These and all other antenna capacity values were measured by the resonance-substitution method suggested in the paragraph on wave-length measurements.

taking several alternate groups of observations consisting of three or five readings each, thus eliminating the effects from any possible change at the sending station. (This method of taking readings was followed in all experiments constituting this investigation unless otherwise specified.) The mean ratios of the galvanometer deflection due to the energy received are to be seen in Table III., as are also the ratios of the current values in each case.

TABLE III.

| System. | Capacity in Microfarads. | Ratio of Gal. Deflections Produced by Various Systems to that Caused by Standard System A. | Ratio of Current Values. (Sq. Root of Gal. Deflection.) |
|---|---|---|---|
| A | 0.000032 | 1.000 | 1.000 |
| B | 0.000056 | 2.220 | 1.488 |
| C | 0.000068 | 2.045 | 1.450 |
| D | 0.000080 | 2.225 | 1.490 |
| E | 0.000060 | 3.520 | 1.880 |

It is apparent from an examination of Table III., that systems, $B$ and $D$, are of practically equal efficiency. $C$, though very close to both $B$ and $D$ in value, showed a persistently lower efficiency. The difference is, however, only slight. It would appear that in erecting multiple-wired antennæ it is practically immaterial whether the component parts are connected at the lower, upper or both ends. Though the metal cylinder shows an apparently greater efficiency than the double-wire type, yet when other obvious factors are considered it is doubtful if such a system possesses any material advantage over the multiple-wire arrangement. The results would also seem to indicate that capacity is not as important a factor in determining the amount of energy received by a given system as is commonly supposed.

In the concluding series of experiments the relative efficiency of several systems already described, together with one or two original arrangements, were tested. The standard of comparison being a single vertical antenna 9.8 m. in length. The systems investigated in these tests were: a large capacity-area 4.2 × .7 m.; a small capacity-area; a large helix, 1.5 m. square, having 12 m. length of wire; a small helix, 15 cm. square, having 12 m. length of wire; a horizontal antenna, 9.8 m. in length; a wire screen, 1

m. square; a special system. The capacity-area, large helix and horizontal antenna were those used in previous experiments. The small helix was made by winding 11.1 m. of wire in 11 turns on a wooden frame 15 × 15 × 11 cm., .9 m. serving as a vertical lead to connect with the horizontal lead at the top of the supporting tripod. The small helix was so arranged that its center was at the same height above the ground as that of the larger helix. The inductance of the smaller coil was .056 milli-henrys. The wire screen

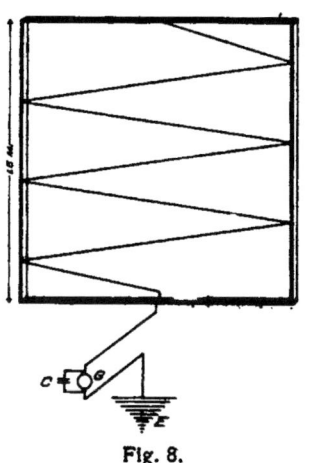

Fig. 8.

consisted of a piece of wire netting, 1 m. square and having a mesh .5 cm. square, fastened to a wooden frame. As in the case of the small capacity-area a vertical wire .75 cm. long connected the middle of the screen to the horizontal lead. The special system consisted of 9.8 m. of wire fastened to a light wooden rectangular frame, in the manner indicated in Fig. 8.

In all cases the systems were carefully insulated from the supporting structures by means of porcelain insulators. As in the tests on orientation, the large capacity and large helix were supported 70 cm. above the surface of the earth at the point of erection, and 16 cm. above the mean level between the two stations. The special system was supported in the same manner. The small capacity-area and the screen were 80 cm. and 25 cm. respectively above the surface and mean level. In the two last mentioned systems 1.5 m. of wire, nearly horizontal, led from the top of the supporting tripod to the lead, $H$. In the case of the large and small helixes and large capacity this connecting wire was 1.7 m. long. Readings were taken in the manner described in the previous experiment. The results are recorded in the following table.

An examination of the above table shows that *all of the receiving systems tested fell far short in efficiency in the matter of intercepting energy when compared with a single vertical wire.* The nearest approach to the vertical wire in the matter of efficiency is made by

TABLE IV.

| System. | Inductance in Milli-henrys. | Capacity in Micro-farads. | Ratio of Gal. Def. Produced by Various Systems to that Caused by Standard. | Ratio of Current Values. |
|---|---|---|---|---|
| Standard vertical antenna. | | 0.000049 | 1.0000 | 1.0000 |
| Large capacity-area. | | 0.000106 | 0.4060 | 0.6360 |
| Small capacity-area. | | 0.000008 (?) | 0.1750 | 0.4190 |
| Large helix. | 0.041 | 0.000044 | 0.2520 | 0.5020 |
| Small helix. | 0.056 | 0.000034 | 0.1060 | 0.3260 |
| Horizontal antenna. | | 0.000340 | 0.1730 | 0.4160 |
| Wire screen. | | 0.000044 | 0.1970 | 0.4440 |
| Special system. | | 0.000030 | 0.2290 | 0.4790 |

the large capacity-area which has an efficiency in current value of a trifle over 63 per cent. It is to be noted, however, that this system has a capacity of more than twice the value of that of the standard antenna. This fact bears out the statement previously made in reference to the effect of capacity in a receiving system. It may also be observed that the horizontal antenna, at least when placed comparatively near the earth, has a relatively small efficiency. The small capacity-area, though only 1 m. square, shows a slightly greater efficiency than the horizontal system, and the wire screen is even still more efficient relatively. The case of the large and small helixes is also of interest. The smaller coil, though having the same length of wire as the larger shows a material falling off in energy received when compared with the larger. This difference may possibly be due to the greater impedance of the smaller helix. When comparing both large and small helixes with the standard type, it is to be remembered that these coils were each made up of 12 m. of wire, while the single wire standard consisted of only 9.8 m. From a practical point of view when length of wire, facility of erection and ease of maintenance are considered the special type shows the greatest efficiency as a receiving system. Its efficiency would probably have been materially increased had its lengths of wire been made to run vertical instead of nearly horizontal.

The resonance curve shown in Fig. 9 above is inserted to show the general properties of the two waves sent out by the sending station. The data for this curve was taken when using the capacity-area 1 m. square as a receiving system. Capacity shunted about the galvanometer is plotted against galvanometer deflections. The lesser maximum probably corresponds to the shorter of the two wave-lengths radiated by the transmitting station and the greater

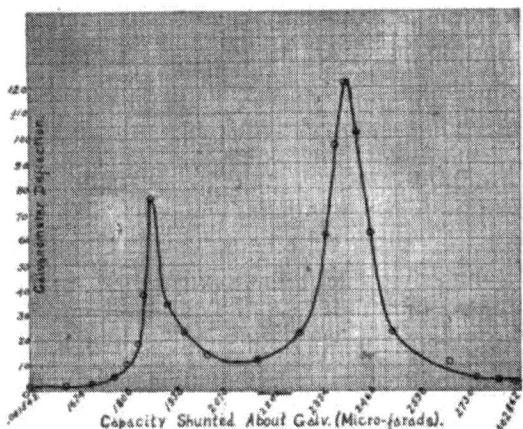

Fig. 9.

maximum to the longer wave-length. However, this relation is somewhat difficult to determine, because of the fact that these maxima would frequently interchange places. The reason for this rather unusual phenomenon we have as yet been unable to determine.

## RESULTS.

To recapitulate, the foregoing data would indicate, under the conditions which obtained in these experiments: (1) that the resistance of the earth between the two stations is an important factor in the propagation of energy; (2) that the square of the energy received by a horizontal antenna is approximately proportional to its length; (3) that relatively small capacity-areas show equal efficiency in all planes of orientation about a vertical axis; (4) that even in the case of capacity-areas whose length is great compared with the width only a slight decrease in efficiency is noticeable when the area is normal to the wave front: (5) that open-circuited helixes are equally efficient in all planes of orientation; (6) that the energy received by such a helix having a given length of wire is a function of its dimensions; (7) that an aërial almost completely screened is but slightly less efficient than a similar unscreened system; (8) that in dealing with multiple-wired antennæ it is practically immaterial as to whether the component parts are connected at the lower, upper or both ends; (9) that in considering different types of receiving systems the actual capacity is not so important as is the manner in which this capacity is distributed; (10) that of the types tested the system consisting of one or more wires normal to the earth's surface is by far the most efficient; (11) that the energy is propagated through the surface of the earth and not by means of a free ether wave.

## DISCUSSION.

The comparative closeness of our stations afforded us a special opportunity to study the effects due to the free Hertzian waves as differentiated from the effects due to the propagation of energy in other possible ways. Stone[1] maintains that the greater portion of the energy transmitted resides in that part of the wave which is immediately adjacent to the surface of the earth. It will be remembered in this connection that our capacity-areas were placed very close to the surface of the earth. If the free wave ever enters as an important factor it should, according to the commonly accepted view, have produced marked effects in our experiments, but, on the contrary, we find in the cases where the capacity-areas, helixes, etc., were rotated about a horizontal axis variation in the plane of orientation produced but slight changes in the amount of energy received, and in some instances resulted in no change whatever. The complete screening of the vertical antenna reduced the received energy but a small per cent. and even this change may have been due to causes other than the shielding effects due to the metal enclosure.

In the experiments having to do with earth resistances the increase in the quantity of energy received was probably not wholly due to the decrease in the resistance between the two stations, but it is reasonable to suppose that the greater part of the increase may be ascribed to this cause.

In view of the facts just enumerated, and since a fixed wavelength and constant supply of energy was radiated from the trans-

[1] Stone, Transactions International Electrical Congress, St. Louis, 1904, p. 558.

mitting station, it would seem that the conclusion is not wholly unwarranted that practically all the energy taking part in wireless telegraph operations is propagated through the surface of the earth by means of electrical oscillations and not by means of free Hertzian waves.

The experience of those engaged in practical wireless work bears out the conclusion of the author in this respect. It is well known that when working over land a slight fall of rain on dry soil materially increases the signalling distance. The fact that it is possible to signal through greater distances over sea than over land we believe to be due to the greater conductivity of the water. The originator of one of the wireless systems now in commercial use informs the writer that in some recent tests made it was found that when operating overland the presence of iron bearing ore in the earth materially increased the signalling distance. Neither the author's experience nor the instance just cited bear out the contention of Sacks[1] who maintains that any good conductor in, or in connection with, the earth is detrimental in its effects. Kimura[2] also holds that the earth resistance does not figure as a factor but that the capacity of the earth plate is the important consideration. The above commercial and theoretical experiments do not tend to confirm this view.

Again, if the theory of a free ether wave is correct, the law of inverse squares should hold, approximately at least. That this law *does not hold* has been shown by several investigators among whom may be mentioned Duddell and Taylor,[3] who found that the product of the distance by the intensity was a constant, and Chant,[4] who also found that the energy fell off inversely as the simple distance.

In considering the possible processes by which energy is propagated in wireless telegraphy it is to be remembered that the beginning of wireless telegraphy as a practical commercial project dates from the time when Marconi first *connected his transmitting apparatus to earth.* The distances over which communication was effected prior to this were insignificant. In fact, until that time the transmission

[1] J. S. Sacks, Ann. der Physik, Vol. 18, p. 348.
[2] Kimura, Phys. Zeitcher, June 29, 1901.
[3] Institute Electrical Engineers Journal, Vol. 35, p. 321.
[4] American Journal of Science, Vol. 18, p. 403.

of intelligence by means of electric waves was little more than an interesting laboratory experiment. In a paper read before the International Electrical Congress, which convened at St. Louis, 1904, Count Solari made the following significant statement: "In other words he (Marconi) made the great discovery that two rods of metal placed *upright in the ground* at some distance apart *form a gigantic and novel oscillator in which electric oscillations set up in the one part are propagated through the earth to the other part*,[1] and at the same time electrical waves formed by the alternations of electric strain directed perpendicularly to the earth and the associated magnetic forces parallel to the earth, are propagated through the ether between the two vertical wires." We hold that the first factor mentioned by the authority just quoted constitutes the vital consideration, and that it was due to this principle that Marconi succeeded in making long distance transmission possible. We do not dispute the existence of the free ether wave but maintain that its effect is nill beyond comparatively short distances from the radiating system.

May we not think of a wireless transmitting apparatus when in operation as impressing upon the earth, at the point where the system is grounded, a high frequency alternating potential, these waves of potential spreading out through the surface of the earth in all directions? If we suppose such a process as taking place, another conductor placed in a vertical position at a distant point and connected either directly or inductively with the surface of the earth would be charged to the oscillating potential represented by the electric earth-wave at that point. Thus we would have the energy transmitted to the receiving system. The resistance of the earth would doubtless diminish the amplitude of the potential wave, hence the importance of high earth conductivity between two stations. It is more than probable that such a potential wave is confined to a very thin stratum of the earth's surface as is maintained by Poincare.[2]

We are aware that at least one empirical fact is difficult of explanation on the basis of the theory which we advance. Professor Fleming quotes the observations of Captain Jackson, of the

---

[1] The italics are ours.
[2] H. Poincare, Bureau des Long. Ann., 1902.

British Navy, relative to the effect of intervening land upon signalling distance, the observation being that hilly or stony ground intervening between two stations greatly decreases the amount of energy transmitted, thus reducing the signalling distance. Lieutenant-commander Robinson of the United States Navy informs the writer that it is a common experience in the Navy to have signals cease almost instantly when an elevated body of land comes to intervene between two vessels or a vessel and a land station. Lieutenant Robinson made the significant remark that "Every hill casts its shadow." We grant this, but we believe that the sudden decrease in energy when passing behind elevated bodies of land can be accounted for on other grounds than that of the electrical shadow in the commonly accepted sense of the term. The author is at present designing a series of experiments by which he hopes to prove this contention.

The phenomenon of the effects of light and darkness upon the propagation of energy we admit is not readily explicable on the assumptions which we advance. However a number of important facts which are difficult to account for upon the idea of a free Hertzian wave become easy of explanation on the basis of the oscillation theory, one notable example being the case of Marconi's Trans-Atlantic communication. This is difficult to explain on the basis of a free ether wave, as is cited by Poincare,[1] but presents no particular difficulty when viewed in the light of the theory outlined above. Notwithstanding the failure of the proposed theory to account for several phenomena encountered in practical wireless work, we believe such a theory accounts for more of the facts now known than the conventional idea of a free energy wave.

RANDAL MORGAN LABORATORY,
    UNIVERSITY OF PENNSYLVANIA,
        May 1, 1907.

[1] H. Poincare, Proc. Roy. Soc., Vol. 72, July 8, 1903.

Printed by Libri Plureos GmbH in Hamburg,
Germany